The BluePrint
a basic plan for discipleship

The BluePrint

Copyright © 2017 Greggory J. Hampton

All rights reserved.

Cover design by Greggory J. Hampton

Cover photo: www.graphicstock.com

ISBN-13: 978-1973787181
ISBN-10: 1973787180

The BluePrint

The BluePrint

CONTENTS

1	You Belong?
2	Next – How to Use This Book
3	Page #1 – REST
4	Page #2 – LIVE at the Table
5	Page #3 – Abide in Prayer
6	Page #4 – Obey God's Word
7	Page #5 – Listen to the Spirit
8	Page #6 – Practice Your Faith
9	Page #7 – Forgive as You're Forgiven
10	Page #8 – WORK with God
11	Your Home Inspection
	BluePrint Bible Verse Plan
	A Closing Prayer of Becoming

The BluePrint

Dedications

To my Father in Heaven: Thank you for offering me rest and life that shapes my work. I'd be a burned down house on a dead end road were it not for your invitation to REST, LIVE, and WORK in a great House.

The BluePrint

Preface

You don't always see the blessing when it's given. And if you are aware enough to see such great love transpiring, you may not yet comprehend the full depth of importance and ongoing impact it will have. I didn't really know what it meant at the time when Mark Calzia took me on a college visit. I didn't know how shaping it would become for Tom Williams to shake my hand and encourage me to sing. I was unaware the impact Jeff Tunberg sharing his guitars with me would have. I didn't know what it would mean to me that Tim Fiscus and George Kalemkarian and Robert Lane taught me God's word in Sunday School each week. I didn't know at the time how important it would be for Michael Umbenhaur to open his back door every time I needed to talk. I could feel that it mattered when Terri Scherer would pray for me and Doug Scherer would speak with words of wisdom into my heart, and I felt loved when Lavon Williams and Rosalie Stoehr would hug me each Sunday morning, but I didn't really *see* the blessing when it was given. I can see now, I wouldn't be who I am were it not for them. They discipled me before I knew what that could be. I find myself in God's house in part because they held open the door. I will cherish them in my heart always. I will carry on what they began.

Greggory J. Hampton
Rock Island, IL
August 17, 2017

Chapter One: BluePrint Introduction
You Belong?

My dad told me a story when I was a young boy about how one of his friends built his own deck on the back of his house. He didn't get a permit and after he had already completed the project, the city inspector caught wind of it and showed up unannounced, with a sledgehammer. The inspector walked around the deck examining the man's work for a few moments and stopped at one of the corners. He lifted his sledgehammer and swung it down a single time on one of the deck's supporting corners. The entire structure fell to the ground with one hit.

My dad's friend bypassed getting permits because he didn't want someone in authority telling him he might need help. He had the ability to build his own deck. He built the whole thing. But he had no idea how to build it to last.

As Christians I think we're sometimes slow to grow because, though we're surrounded by opportunities for growth, we don't actually know how to participate with a plan. Like my Dad's friend, we don't want someone telling us what to do. We can hammer two boards together just fine by ourselves, but we don't know how to build a deck so it doesn't fall down with one hit. For some reason we still think we can do it on our own.

If this sounds like you, you may not like this book because it's going to tell you what to do. Or maybe the inspector just left your house and you can see your deck in pieces on the ground, all your hard work for nothing, and you've realized you might need some help. In that case, you might need this book very much.

Open a Bible to the book of Ephesians, chapter 2 beginning in verse 19 (I especially like this in the Message version). You'll find words describing how God is using each of us to build a home. We aren't cast out. We're not alone. We're no longer strangers and wanderers. If we believe in Jesus, it is in Jesus we have found a home. It is in Jesus we find belonging. And if we believe in Jesus, he is making each of us a part of a new home. He's building something none of us could build. He is, piece by piece, putting together a miraculous mansion, somehow majestic beyond imagination, welcoming the greatest and least into the same house.

You might feel the Ephesians 2 passage resonating in your heart. But maybe that doesn't sound like you because you've never believed with your mind or spoken with your mouth that you believe in Jesus as your God. But it can resonate, and it can start right now!

Say this as a Prayer of Belonging to God:

> Oh God our Heavenly Father, I am finding I want to be in your family. I am finding I want to belong in you. I know I have made mistakes. I have sinned, and thought I couldn't belong. But now I believe Jesus is your Son, that he died for my sins, and has given me life, forever, in your family. Now I can see my mistakes and sin can't keep you away from me. You have found me. You have forgiven me. You have told me I belong in your family. And I believe you. Amen.

You belong! You are a part of God's family. You are being built into the home and house that God is building. Integrally placed. Intentionally loved.

If this is new for you, a next step you can take is to find out when you can be baptized with water in your local church! When you are baptized, three very basic things happen: You *confirm* that you believe in Jesus. Jesus *affirms* that you are a part of his family. And you *inform* the world what you believe about the church, namely that we don't "belong" on our own — we belong together.

So why has this first chapter been about following a plan, and believing in Jesus, and baptism? Because this is a book about discipleship, and knowing you belong in God, and believing in Jesus, and being baptized is just the beginning of discipleship.

What comes next in discipleship is being built into a house, together. And with any house, there's a blueprint. There's a plan. This book is one plan, one way, a blueprint for discipleship.

Now, if you're the guy that skips getting permits for your new deck, you may also be the kind of person that skips using a blueprint of discipleship to be shaped into the likeness of Jesus. You just wing it and wonder why after years you don't feel much more like Jesus than when you began. But Brennan Manning in *The Ragamuffin Gospel* (Chapter 10, The Victorious Limp, pg. 176) says, "What makes authentic disciples is not visions, ecstasies, biblical mastery of chapter and verse, or spectacular success in ministry, but a capacity for faithfulness."

I hope you'll come along for this imposed plan. With a little faithfulness, you'll turn the pages of the BluePrint and see what could be.

The BluePrint

The BluePrint

Chapter Two: Next
How to Use This Book

Some years ago I built a table. If you know me at all, this is a very surprising fact. My wife decided to do more homeschooling and needed a table for the boys to sit at, so I decided I'd build it myself instead of spending a bunch of money on one from the store. Sounds smart, right?

I went to Lowe's and bought one solid piece of wood to use for the top of the table, some boards to use as legs and support under the table, and I went home to begin building in my garage. It probably only took me about ninety minutes to put it all together. And while many of my stories involve me accidentally injuring myself, I didn't lose any fingers while cutting the different pieces to size, so that's a bonus! Immediately after the table was all put together I felt this great sense of accomplishment. "I did that!" I thought. "Who needs instructions? My kids will learn awesome things at that table for years to come," I told myself.

We no longer have the table. Pieces of it fell off. It wasn't square. Day-by-day, week-by-week, and month-by-month, I began to notice all of its insufficiencies. The way the legs were just slightly different lengths. The way the angled supports would jut out in spots that should be flush. The way, you know, again, the pieces fell off. When we moved across town, the table did not move with us.

The sense of accomplishment was gone. This happens to many new and older Christians alike. There is an initial rush of joy and satisfaction in knowing Jesus. And then life happens. Things fall apart, and we don't always understand why.

Some people can build without a blueprint, not because they've *never* used one, but because they *have* used one so often and built so many things, they've learned how to build just about anything imaginable. The point is, initially, they had plans that were imposed for each build, and now they can improvise.

The BluePrint is meant to be like this. It is meant to be a pattern of discipleship we impose on our lives until the pattern becomes natural and consistent enough to be improvised. This book is meant to help make sure you don't build something that will be easily dismantled and discarded.

So what is the BluePrint? Simply, it is to "REST, LIVE, and WORK in a great House." And that can be broken down further to look like this:

Saturday	- REST in the Father
Sunday	- LIVE at the Table
Monday	- Abide in Prayer
Tuesday	- Obey God's Word
Wednesday	- Listen to the Spirit
Thursday	- Practice your Faith
Friday	- Forgive as you're Forgiven
Any Time	- WORK with God

We'll spend the rest of this book laying out the pages of this BluePrint so you can see each layer and how it is meant to come together. Each chapter will focus on one piece of the pattern. Logistically speaking, you can choose to read one chapter each week, or at your own pace. At the end of each chapter there will be action items on how to participate with what you've read, how to build on the BluePrint, and space to take notes or journal.

Additionally, you'll have eight weeks worth of scriptures you can look up and read to reinforce the pattern of the BluePrint each day. There is one verse for every day for each subject, with an extra verse for WORK. Eight verses each week for a total of 64 verses.

No matter the pace you pick, I hope you see that as you follow the pattern, the pattern will start following you. Impose it and you'll end up able to improvise it. You'll see it in your life, and you'll be able to intentionally live out your discipleship.

PARTICIPATE

Option 1 – On ANY day, start by reading Page One (Chapter Three). Then go through Scripture Week #1 at the back of the book one day at a time. I've chosen Saturday as the default day the pattern can begin but you can start any day.

The next week on the same day, read the

next chapter. Then go through Scripture Week #2. And so on for 8 weeks.

I find it most effective to choose the same day each week to read a chapter and then have a consistent time each day when you open your Bible and read the scripture for that day. You might notice I don't print out the text of the verses I reference in this book. This is intentional. Practice opening your Bible and finding these passages.

Option 2 – You could read the book straight through more quickly, still use the scriptures over the course of eight weeks, and check back on each chapter as a reminder.

Option 3 – Read a chapter and instead of reading the corresponding scripture week as listed, spend a week or more studying and reading the one verse from each of the eight weeks that pertain directly to that topic (for example, read REST, then study all eight verses on REST). In this way, you will go deeper into a topic all at once before moving on to the next idea. For your convenience, all eight scripture weeks are grouped together at the end of the book.

Ok. Here we go. Let's start with Page One of the BluePrint. REST.

The BluePrint

The BluePrint

Chapter Three: BluePrint Page One
REST

In God's BluePrint, rest comes first. I believe this deeply. If you've never heard that before, hear it now. Rest comes first. Not last.

When I was 23 years old I was working three jobs. I was a part-time youth pastor at a Baptist church, an intern with a young adult ministry at a Wesleyan church, and a full-time teacher's aid at a daycare. On top of all this I was dating Cynthia (my now wife), and applying for full-time ministry work. It was the first time I felt I was really working hard, adopting a whatever-it-takes attitude. All together I was working 60+ hours a week. I was tired. But I was doing a lot for God! So I figured it's what God wanted. Right?

One Friday, in the late afternoon, I was

driving on John Deere Rd, a main highway that connects different parts of the area where I live, in my old gray Oldsmobile Firenza. I was so tired in every way. Mentally, emotionally, physically. I pulled up and stopped at a red light on this busy highway and the next thing I know I'm being startled awake by traffic speeding past me. I don't remember falling asleep. I do remember feeling very lucky I kept my foot on the brakes. I also remember being thankful no one rear-ended me doing 55mph.

Has that ever happened to you? Is that happening to you right now? You're working so hard you're falling asleep when you should be most alert? Have you ever felt this way about your relationship with Jesus or your involvement at church? Unfortunately, too often, church isn't a place of rest for people. Church can become a place to be worked so hard you're too tired to know how to not be tired. You can feel like everything you're doing is so very important, and when everything feels important, everything can feel like work. And when everything feels like work, resentment can follow closely after.

Resentment is kind of like when you want the paycheck, but you hate the boss. Or maybe you like the job and the boss, but you harbor a grudge against the company. You can start to feel this way when you've said yes to too many things too many times. You might even remember really wanting to do this, but now you're upset you have to get up at 6am to go to work. You resent it. You're so tired even your rest feels like work. We get to a place where nothing feels like rest and we develop a film of guilt around the times of rest we are able to find.

The great news I've learned and I hope you hear is that rest is required in being a disciple. We are told and called to begin focusing on rest, because rest has a place and important position in our life.

Open up a Bible to Matthew 11. In Matthew 11 we see something amazing. Look at verses 28-30. Jesus says if we come to him he will give us work? No, he says he will give us rest!

In the day Jesus originally said this there was something called the "yoke of the law." It was a way of following God that had become unbearably heavy, so heavy that no one could possibly do it all. In this passage and in your life, Jesus is offering a "lighter" way, a way that doesn't first focus on the rules, but on the rest. The first thing Jesus calls us to is to put down the un-Christ like work we have been doing, the law-driven, get-it-right-the-first-time kind of work, and rest first in him. I love this! Rest is first.

Learn this phrase and repeat it or pray it over and over: "Jesus, you are my peace, you are my true rest." Breathe in, say "Jesus, you are my peace." Breathe out and say "You are my true rest."

Work will eventually come. Jesus will also give us work. Yes. But work will never be healthy unless rest has come first. Listen, rest is not a reward for work. Work is the result of life-giving rest.

Turn one more place in your Bible. Psalm 127:1-2b (the "b" just means the second half of the verse). What does it say? It says God blesses us, gives to us, provides what we need, even while we sleep. I don't know about you, but I am worthless when I'm asleep, dead to the world. My wife will regularly ask if I heard the storm that battered our home in the middle of the night and my answer is always the same, no. And yet, when I am helpless, this is when God gives me what I need.

The point is this: God's favor, and provision, are not the result of our great work, they are the result of his great love. You don't have to do anything to earn rest. So take a deep breath and let the rest of God begin.

PARTICIPATE

Prayer for REST

Oh God our Heavenly Father
Give us rest
Let peace be where we find you
Let the hurry and frustrations
Of our every day life be calmed
And resolved in you
May our hearts be overwhelmed
Not with worry, but with you
Let control be released
May your beauty take its place
Rest, Peace, Relief
Thank you for these. Amen.

BUILD

Turn to the Week #1 Scriptures in the back of the book and read each passage on the coinciding or consecutive days.

Continue reading Page Two of the BluePrint now, or come back next week.

Consider putting a reminder in your calendar for Saturdays: "Today is a day to REST."

The BluePrint

The BluePrint

Chapter Four: BluePrint Page Two
LIVE at the Table

In 2007 my wife and I bought a little antique farm table for our kitchen from a small shop outside of a little town called Braselton, GA. At the time we only had one son and another on the way, so a three-foot by four-foot table was more than enough. It had a beautiful patina and green hazy tint. I wondered how many families had owned it, and how many people had eaten how many meals around it? We loved that table.

Eight years later in 2015, Cynthia and I now had four kids, and as we moved into our current home we knew the old farm table would no longer be big enough for the whole family. We had been jamming all of us around the old table, but now was the time. My friend Ken Westbrooks lives in Georgia near the same town our first table was purchased, so I commissioned him to build and ship us a custom eight-foot by three-foot farm table of our very own. It's a beautiful table, and we're the only ones that have ever owned it. But we're not the only ones that have eaten around this table. We've had many people join us for meals and memory making around our table.

There's something special about a table. There is something even more special about being at a table, together.

In the Old Testament of the Bible there are many descriptions of gifts and sacrifices given to our God. They were given for the sake of forgiveness and reconciliation. But they were given and offered on altars, not tables, so why do we live 'at a table' and not at the altar?

On the night that Jesus was betrayed, he broke the bread and blessed the cup and said they symbolized his body and his blood that would offer forgiveness once for all and create the only way for reconciliation with God and each other. He did this while sharing a sacred meal, seated at a table with his disciples. The bread broken and wine given, representatives of his very own body and blood, were on the table. You could say

Jesus put everything on the table for us, and in a way, showed us the altar and the table are now one in the same.

When we belong and believe, and when we accept his rest, we begin to learn what it means to live in Jesus. We find to truly live, we must lay everything down, just like Jesus. We have to put everything on the table. We do this with God, and we do this with each other at the table.

Have you put everything on the table? Your future? Your hopes? Your desires? Your dreams? And the less ambiguous things, like your sexuality? Your money? Your words? Your thoughts? Your relationships?

The very first step after rest, to live in Jesus, is to die to yourself. Put everything on the table and be nourished, not with your own desires, your own impulses, or your own nature, but with the very body and blood of Jesus. His work on the cross offers you rest. What he put on the table offers you life.

I want you to imagine a table before you. Maybe you're sitting at a table right now. Imagine yourself placing everything about yourself on that table.

There are going to be some things that Jesus

wants to take off of the table because they're sinful and hurtful and breaking you.

There are going to be things Jesus will push toward you and trust you with, saying, "Here, eat this, this is good for you."

There may be things Jesus will leave on the table, pulled to the corner, out of reach, because you're not yet mature or wise enough to handle them, saying, "This is for later."

Jesus may even leave a struggle, challenge, or frustration, on the table. After all, how will you ever learn to trust him if there's nothing still on the table that requires trust? Think about it, the salt is always on the table at a restaurant, but we almost never need more salt.

Nothing is ever, ever, taken off the table by us. We put it on the table, and Jesus sets what we need before us, only what we need, when we need it. It reminds me of a quote from *The Adventures of the Brothers Brave and Noble*. The young protagonist is told this new world he's found himself in will provide, "Whatever is needed, whenever it's needed."

When we put everything we have on the table, we free ourselves to accept everything Jesus has put on the table. And what he has is so much better. It's a life we couldn't give ourselves. It's a life we all long to live, but are completely incapable of producing or providing, even in the slightest form, from our own strength. When we put everything on the table and live in Jesus, we find by his grace we are prepared for the trials that will come that much more. Why? Because now the energy and wisdom found within us isn't stored up from anything we have done, but from everything HE has done. And when we put everything on the table we find we aren't alone at the table.

Consider looking up Galatians 2:20, and Galatians 6:2. These verses offer us a new perspective on life. A life born out of dying. Dying to self. Putting everything on the table, holding nothing back. And in this, we find something surprising, a family that shares a common victory with us. It's an odd victory. It's a victory we can't own alone or only personally claim. It's actually a victory we carry collectively. When we lay down our burdens, our new family at the table take them up. And so together we have victory.

Think of it like this: In the summer of 2017 I served as a camp counselor at Royal Family Kids camp, a camp for kids in foster care. Every meal was amazing, and the priority was always the kids. If there was one dinner roll left and a counselor reached for it, their hand might get swiped away to make sure the kids had the chance to fill their bellies first. Malnutrition is a common reality for these kids prior to being placed in foster care, so they are sometimes smaller than other kids their age. And as much as we loved these kids, there would be moments when one of us counselors would lose sight of why we were there. In these moments we'd need to be reminded. We'd need our hand brushed away from something we wanted in favor of providing what these amazing kids needed.

When we live at the table we help each other leave things on the table we don't need to hold onto ourselves, while letting someone else with a greater need be nourished. Of course, a beautiful thing about God's family is there's always enough of exactly what's needed for everyone at the table (check out 1 Thessalonians 5:14 and James 5:16).

Take the time to consider, is your table bare? Have you put it all on the table? Not only for you, but also for others? The more we put on the table, the more we are filled with what God has on the table, and the more we will naturally connect with God and others.

Over the next five chapters we will continue to unpack what it means to LIVE in Jesus.

PARTICIPATE

Prayer to LIVE

Oh Living God, we want to live
There is no other one that gives life
There is no other that conquers death
Conquer death in us
And replace it with your life
Lead us away from all
That steals and kills and destroys
And instead lead us into
Life-to-the-full
Life
That is what you have for us. Amen.

BUILD

Turn to the Week #2 Scriptures and read each passage on the coinciding day.

Continue reading Page Three of the BluePrint now, or come back in a week after going through all of Week #2's scriptures.

To build on the BluePrint, consider putting a reminder in your calendar or phone for every Sunday called "Today is a day to LIVE."

The BluePrint

The BluePrint

Chapter Five: BluePrint Page Three
Abide in Prayer

For three summers as a teenager, I would spend every day at the park playing tennis, at least for the first month or so before I'd fizzle out. I didn't go because of great equipment, and it wasn't because there were other kids. I went because of Al. Al was an 80 year old man that would ride his bike, from where he lived in a second floor apartment, midway down 23rd Avenue, to Browning Park at the corner of 23rd and 16th in Moline, IL. Every year Al would get the nets out of the storage facility at the park and he'd put them up so people could play tennis. He'd sit there on the bench at the side of the first of two courts, drinking water out of an old tennis-ball can, and he would take care of the courts. He also did what he could to care for the players that would play, all easily younger than him by 20 or 30 years.

Al wasn't a fantastic player, but there was never a day I beat him in a full set of tennis. I could serve faster than him. I could hit harder. Even as a 13 year old, I could hit a stinging forehand, and a stronger backhand. But Al watched the ball better than I did, and he could place it anywhere he wanted.

A few years ago I started playing tennis at the club here in town every once in a while because my friend was one of the pros and needed a sub for a league he ran. One of the other pros asked me about my serving motion, "How did you get it so fluid? It's nice to watch." I told him about Al.

Al taught me that my whole body was involved when I would serve. You don't just throw the ball into the air and swing. Your swinging motion is a part of the toss. As your feet move and your knees bend, your body extends and stretches from your toes to the tip of your racket. All of this body motion and energy wind up like a spring for the moment the strings will come into contact with the ball.

But you can have a very pretty motion and

still have a very bad serve. Believe me, I've shanked more than my fair share directly over the fence. The key Al taught me? The whole time, you must look at the ball, and nothing else. This is why he always won.

If that isn't a picture of abiding prayer, I don't know what is. The importance of prayer cannot be overstated. The great value of prayer isn't simply found in the amount of time or the words we say. Our prayers don't have to be long and they don't have to be fancy. Prayer is effective when prayer is essentially about one thing, keeping our eyes on God. And then, time in prayer will shape us.

Read John 14:16-20. Jesus is talking about a level of connectedness with him, the Father, and the Spirit that would soon arrive. When we spend time in prayer, this is the connectedness we are fostering. We are focusing our eyes on God and being shaped by the time we spend embracing the abiding presence of God.

And while it isn't about the amount of time, time is required. Abiding is a promise given by Jesus, but it takes some intentionality on our part to experience the depth of that promise. I had to get up every day during those summer months, fill my water jug, grab my racket, hop on my bike (awkwardly holding the jug and racket over the top of my handlebars), and ride the half-mile to the park along a marginally busy street. All of this took time. Setting time aside to abide in prayer is insurmountably more important than time spent playing tennis. Time isn't important because it creates our connection with God, but because it opens our awareness to the connectedness that is already promised when we believe in Jesus. It puts our eye on the ball. It allows space for us to be shaped. It opens the door to the depths of connectedness with God that is promised in prayer.

We turn our eyes toward God in our time of prayer and find our eyes can be trained to stay there. Fizzle happens. I never made it to the courts every day of an entire summer. You may fail to abide at all times, but God is present to us every moment in every season. We may fizzle. He does not.

PARTICIPATE

Take a moment. Take a deep breath. Close your eyes. Begin by thinking about God already being present, abiding with you. Choose to abide with God.

BUILD

Turn to the Week #3 Scriptures in the back of the book and read each passage on the coinciding day.

Continue reading Page Four of the BluePrint now, or come back in a week after going through all of Week #3's scriptures.

To build on the BluePrint, consider putting a reminder in your calendar or phone for every Monday called "Today is a day to Abide."

The BluePrint

The BluePrint

Chapter Six: BluePrint Page Four
Obey God's Word

Do you remember when an oxygen tank exploded aboard NASA's Apollo 13 Mission? I don't either. I wasn't born yet. But I've seen the movie and I've read the Wikipedia page.

When the crew of the Apollo 13 had to abort their plans to land on the moon, they also had to adopt a new plan to survive. In a kind of ironic reversal, the people floating in the heavens had to obey their team on earth. If they didn't do exactly what they were directed to do, the chance of surviving would shrink to zero. Not to spoil the movie, or history, but they survived and made it back to earth. They obeyed. They lived.

Garvin McCarrell told me, "You can't correct until you instruct." Garvin is one of my spiritual overseers. I don't know how many times

I've asked him a question and heard him say, "Well, it's like this..." and then sound advice shaped by scripture comes pouring out.

There's never been a time that Garvin just told me what I had to do, but I've always seemed to know what to do after we talk. He's never asked me to obey his instruction, and yet I find myself following his insight time and again. Where does he get his wisdom? Life-experience? Sure. But I know his true foundation is God's word. Garvin has been instructed by the Bible. He has learned to obey in the best sense of the word.

Each of us has probably felt like a crewmember of Apollo 13 at one point or another. Something explodes in our life, our plans are scrapped, and we have to adjust to survive. But we aren't floating in space and we don't have a Mission Control of nearly 150 people working three shifts around the clock to solve our problems. However, we do have a Bible inspired by the God of the heavens, written by more than 40 people, with 66 books, nearly 1200 chapters, and over 31,000 verses. And we have each other, people like Garvin. We have the Church, a living breathing mission control that can help us understand the Bible and obey it.

But why is it important to obey the Bible? Open your Bible and read John 14:21. We see two basic things here: A challenge and a reward. We're challenged to understand that obeying God is what shows that we love God. And we see a reward. If we obey and show our love for the father, then we will know the love of the father for us.

Maybe that sounds like a "works" mentality. Maybe it doesn't seem fair that we should have to obey God in order to show we actually love God. On the other hand, it's odd to me how often we don't do for God what we expect everyone else around us to do for us.

If you were in a relationship and he or she said, "I don't think I'll do anything that pleases you ever again and you'll just have to believe that I love you," we'd be like, "say what?" None of us would call that love. None of us would feel satisfied with that. Is it not right that God hopes we will show our love for him? Is it not right that love be shown in obedience? And after all, aren't we the ones that actually benefit from obedience? When we obey, showing our love for the father, in turn, we will receive the great reward of knowing the love of the father for us.

Is it an ultimatum? If you obey, then and only then you will be loved? I don't think so. It is revelation. When you obey, you will become aware of what is already true, that God loves you.

This passage in John isn't telling us God doesn't love us unless we obey every time. What I believe we're seeing here is that our obedience toward God reveals and opens our eyes to his love that is already there. And it's not that God is hiding his love, as much as we have layers and layers of blindness covering his love. And one of the greatest ways to remove our layers of blindness is obedience.

You could put it this way: Obedience leads to seeing God's love, and seeing God's love leads us to obedience. So how do we obey? We obey by reading his word and allowing his word to shape our lives.

PARTICIPATE

If you haven't already, begin using the scriptures in the back of this book. Read them, and consider how to obey. When you obey God's word, it will build on your time of prayer and abiding. Use your growing prayer life to encourage your growing life of obedience in God's word. Make one of your prayers when you practice abiding, "God, help me read your word and obey."

BUILD

Turn to the Week #4 Scriptures and read each passage on the coinciding day.

Continue reading Page Five of the BluePrint now, or come back in a week after going through all of Week #4's scriptures.

To build on the BluePrint, consider putting a reminder in your calendar or phone for every Tuesday called "Today is a day to Obey."

The BluePrint

The BluePrint

Chapter Seven: BluePrint Page Five
Listen to the Spirit

You may not know this about me, but I'm hilarious. I have proof. Many years ago I went to open auditions for something called Comedy Sportz, a kind of competitive improv group. My buddy Eric convinced me to go because he wanted to audition but didn't want to go alone. It was only a little awkward later that evening when I got a call back and Eric did not. But, we're still friends today, so all is well. I'm just funnier. At least that's what I maintain.

Truth is, improv is less about being funny and more about being a good listener. I remember in the audition, they had me sit in a chair with a person on either side of me. I had to look at the first person and tell them about a subject like space travel, while the second person on the other side of me was talking to me about an entirely different subject, like the process of milking a cow. They'd say "switch" and I'd have to turn to the second person and tell them everything they'd told me about milking a cow. To make things more difficult, while I'm talking about cows now, the first person is talking to me about an entirely new subject like the many different kinds of juggling techniques. They'd say "switch" again and now I had to turn and talk about juggling while being barraged with yet another new subject from behind.

I wasn't asked to be funny. I was tested on whether I could listen. The reason listening is so important to improv comedy is because listening speaks to our awareness, and awareness creates the space for great improv. Interestingly enough, awareness is also what's required to listen to the Spirit of God.

Open your Bible to John 14:26, 27. Jesus tells us the Spirit will teach us and remind us everything Jesus taught. Ok. But what if we aren't listening? What if we aren't aware? What if there's a world full of people behind us talking in our ear about cow juggling astronauts and we're having a hard time paying attention to what God might me trying to tell us. Remember, I have four kids. I can be speaking directly to one of them, right to their face with our eyes locked, and not be confident they heard every word I said.

So how do we listen? Shhhhhhhhh. Slow down for just a tick. While it's true the Spirit will speak in very specific moments about very specific things, I also believe it's true that the Spirit of God is always speaking. You don't have to worry about missing what the Spirit is saying. God is infinite, meaning he exists at all times, not only the moment that felt important to you. What God's Holy Spirit may have to say to you right now will be available two minutes from now. So let go of the false worry, the fear of missing out.

That's not to say you should intentionally put off listening until later. But you can have enough grace for yourself to not beat yourself up if you feel like you missed an important moment.

Ok, now I'm listening. I'm relaxing into this and letting go of being scared I might miss something. But now, how do I know what I might hear is the Spirit? The easiest thing I can say is this: The Spirit sounds like the Bible.

Let me play this out a bit more. When you practice the weekly pattern we've been moving through, you will be ready to hear. If you slow down and accept rest from God. If you die to yourself, putting everything on the table and let God set your life before you. If you pray and begin talking to God. If you read his words and seek to obey. Then when you quiet your mind and listen for the Spirit, you will be prepared to hear, and you will hear that the Spirit sounds a whole lot like the Bible you've already been reading.

How do you know you're hearing the Spirit? The Spirit will never tell you something the Bible doesn't already say or reinforce. And so we're back to listening and awareness. You may not be able to effectively listen to the Spirit if you aren't seeking to be actively aware of what he has already said.

Do you want to hear the Spirit? Train yourself to know what kinds of things the Spirit will say by reading what the Spirit has already said. Read your Bible and seek to obey. His voice will suddenly become singular, instead of an echoing conversation.

One last piece of insight about listening to

the Spirit. Listen to the Spirit by listening to your godly friends. There may be times when you fizzle. You might pray and feel your words are hitting a wall. You may open your Bible and feel you're reading the dictionary. You may listen with full awareness and hear crickets. In these moments, we listen from the table. We listen with others. We listen to others. I'll leave you with a quote that I love from *Life Together* by Dietrich Bonhoeffer:

> "Therefore, the Christian needs another Christian who speaks God's Word to him. He needs him again and again when he becomes uncertain and discouraged, for by himself he cannot help himself without belying the truth… He needs his brother solely because of Jesus Christ. The Christ in his own heart is weaker than the Christ in the word of his brother; his own heart is uncertain, his brother's is sure."

PARTICIPATE

Consider participating in something as simple as a listening prayer. Richard Foster describes "Palms Down, Palms Up" in his book *Celebration of Discipline*:

> "Begin by placing your palms (facing) down as a symbolic indication of your desire to turn over any concerns you may have to God... Whatever it is that weighs on your mind or is a concern to you... release it... After several moments of surrender, turn your palms up as a symbol of your desire to receive from the Lord... spend the remaining moments in complete silence. Do not ask for anything. Allow the Lord to commune with you, to love you."

When you have let go of what you don't need to hold onto and opened your hands to the Lord, in this silent space, listen for the Spirit to speak.

BUILD

Turn to the Week #5 Scriptures and read each passage on the coinciding day.

Continue reading Page Six of the BluePrint now, or come back in a week after going through all of Week #5's scriptures.

To build on the BluePrint, put a reminder in your calendar or phone for every Wednesday called "Today is a day to LISTEN to the Spirit."

The BluePrint

The BluePrint

Chapter Eight: BluePrint Page Six
Practice Your Faith

Brent-Anthony Johnson (BAJ) is the single best bassist I know. Hands down. And I know a few truly great bassists. Go to Google or YouTube and type in his full name and you'll get page after page of videos and articles from BAJ, and you will be impressed. But it's not just his natural ability or talent that makes him a great bassist. BAJ does something almost no other musician that I've met, or that I know, still does. BAJ has been playing the bass for 40 years and he still practices every day.

When I was a young boy, my mom put me in piano lessons. I complained my way out of them and to this day I wish I knew how to play the piano. Now I just plunk around and pretend to know what I'm doing. Maybe you play the bass, or maybe you play the piano, but I'm pretty sure if you're eight chapters into this book you're most likely a Christian. So my question is this: Do you have a faith in God that you practice every day? I'm not asking if you preach sermons daily, or lead worship each morning, or have a quota for leading co-workers and neighbors to the Lord. Do you practice your faith each day?

As a bassist, BAJ is the epitome of having imposed practice in a way that allows improvisation to become second nature. One of the primary reasons BAJ is such an exceptional bassist and plays in a way that very few can, is because every day he plays in the same way that anyone could. He practices.

In many ways, being discipled and practicing your faith is like learning an instrument. It's a lot like what BAJ does every day with his bass. If you don't practice what you are learning, what you're reading, and what you're hearing, you'll get years down the road and wonder why you don't have a grasp on your craft. And in your life in Jesus, if you don't practice what you're learning, reading, or hearing, you will get years down the road and wonder what the shape of your life would be like if you had practiced your faith in Jesus Christ more consistently.

Open your Bible and read John 15:1-5. Jesus tells us that we will grow with him, but we will also be pruned. I believe pruning happens when we practice. I had a high school choir teacher that would say, "If you sing it wrong the first time you read it wrong. Sing it wrong the second time and you learned it wrong." You have to sing it out to know if you were signing it correctly. And you have to sing it loud enough for the director to tell you if you're on the right track.

I'm not joking when I say I was at an elementary school band concert and a kid holding a violin in the front row was literally pretending to play his violin the entire time. The bow was easily six inches off the strings. How do you improve if you don't take the risk of playing some wrong notes?

Pruning happens in practice, and if no one has ever told you, you need to know that you have permission to make mistakes. Even in the example Jesus uses with the vine, we should hear Jesus telling us that we're allowed time to get things right. It would take up to three years for a new vine to bear fruit, and that was only after precise and intentional pruning. You don't have to get it right the first time. You just have to be willing to continually try.

Good fruit doesn't always show up the first season. Musicians are rarely exceptional in their first year of playing. Christians don't fully reflect Jesus right away.

So how do we practice? What is the first thing that comes to your mind when I ask, "What do you think God wants you to practice?" No matter how small, do that. It might be something as small as posting a Bible verse image on your social media for your friends and family to see. It might be speaking to one of your friends or family directly about who Jesus is. It might be privately praying for the healing of a neighbor. It might be speaking a word of encouragement to a co-worker. Whatever it is, do it, and have grace for the mistake.

There's one last thing I'd like to say about practicing our faith. Not every church knows how to let people practice. Not every church knows how to prune in a way that's helpful. This is true. There are many who have left the church because they've been abused in some way. I remember becoming a student in the New Life

School of Worship after a particularly hard season in ministry. I told the school director, Glenn Packiam, "Thank you for accepting me into the school." Glenn said, "Thank you for not giving up on ministry after what you've been though."

Not every church knows how to prune effectively. Conversely, not every churchgoer knows the difference between a helpful pruning cut, and an act of abuse. Both hurt. Both will cause us to want to recoil or pull back. But in my view, too often, people run from the church when they've been pruned, believing they've been abused. I hope you will explore the difference between healthy cuts and abusive acts. Abusive acts are inexcusable. They are undeniably against God's heart, and very well may lead you to a new church family. But don't give up, because, healthy cuts will lead you to life and take you deeper into the family you're meant to be in, if you stay through the pain.

It is difficult to accept correction, I know. Mistakes will be made. Pruning will happen. And pruning hurts. But pruning happens when we practice and there is no growth without practicing our faith.

PARTICIPATE

Add on to the Palms Down, Palms Up prayer from the last chapter. This time, in the time of letting go intentionally let go of all that hinders you from practicing your faith. In the time with your palms up to receive from God, hear and receive from God something specific he would like you to practice with an action.

BUILD

Turn to the Week #6 and read each passage on the coinciding day.

Continue reading Page Seven of the BluePrint now, or come back in a week after going through all of Week #6's scriptures.

Create a reminder for every Thursday called "Today is a day to Practice my Faith."

The BluePrint

The BluePrint

Chapter Nine: BluePrint Page Seven
Forgive as You're Forgiven

I grew up in the same house from three months to 18 years of age. My parents still live there now. It's a 1½-story house with three bedrooms, one bathroom, a two-butt kitchen, half a basement, and aluminum siding. In the 40 years my parents have lived in that little blue house they've made some big improvements: new windows, two new roofs, central air conditioning, a remodeled bathroom, new floors, a new two-car garage, an additional bedroom, a drop ceiling, a new coat closet. My dad even had the foundation walls reinforced this past year. There have been 40 years worth of improvements.

Do you know one thing my parents have never had to replace or improve? The aluminum siding. That house has a strong shell. I don't know how many storms it has lived through, but I do remember one day as a kid, before we had the two-car garage, when it hailed so badly that my dad had to get all the dents in his '82 Buick LeSabre repaired. The siding on the house? It was fine. That siding seems almost indestructible.

I think in life we're tempted to cover ourselves in something like aluminum siding. Even as a pastor, I've been told that if I want to make it over the long haul I have to have thick skin, I have to put on a Kevlar flak jacket. But there's a problem. I like the idea of aluminum siding on a house that leaves no marks even after a hail storm, but I can't stand the thought of living a life that is in no way effected by the difficult things that might happen to me?

Why? Because if I'm unaffected, I'm no longer breathing. It's fine for my parents' house to have siding that seemingly can't be dented by a major hailstorm. But my parents' house is an inanimate object. The house of my life is a living breathing thing. What we're building here with the BluePrint is meant to be strong, but it's not meant to be impenetrable. It isn't adamantine. It is flesh and blood.

Open your Bible and read John 15:12-15. One day I was with Jared Moore, a pastor friend of mine, and I wondered out loud, "maybe it's what we hold back that makes us lonely." I had been thinking about what Jesus said in John 15:12-15. Here he is, Jesus is with his disciples and he calls them friends. He tells them they're friends because he's held nothing back. And he tells them there is no greater act of friendship than laying down your life. Within the next day or so, Jesus would be nailed to a cross.

For some reason we make Jesus's declaration of friendship and his act of laying down his life for our forgiveness, two completely separate and autonomous things. His great declaration and his crucifixion happen within hours of each other but we keep them sanitarily separate. So let me boil it down and say it as clearly as I think it should be understood. When Jesus says, "Greater love has no one than this: to lay down one's life for one's friends," what we must understand is that there is no friendship without forgiveness and there is no forgiveness without dying.

In Jesus, to forgive is to lay down your life.

To lay down your life is to forgive. When did we get the idea we could forgive in some disembodied way that requires no life laid down? We're walking around with aluminum siding, with Kevlar covered hearts. And then we wonder why we're lonely. If what we hold back is what keeps us lonely, I believe forgiveness is the single greatest thing we are holding back, and it's not only making us lonely, it's keeping us from growing in Jesus.

So why do we hold it back? Because, in holding back forgiveness, we think we're holding onto life. But we've already established, if we are going to live with Jesus, we have to put everything on the table, we have to be willing to die, in order to live. We've all heard it said, "Not forgiving someone is like drinking poison expecting the other person to die." So will you die from not forgiving, or will you choose your own death, and willingly forgive, simultaneously offering and receiving a more valuable life.

Keep this in mind. The same way you need nails to die on a cross, you need nails to build a house. Not forgiving is like trying to build a house without nails, and then it won't matter what kind of siding you have because it will never stand. When Jesus died, it took at least three nails to hold him to his cross. How many will it take to hold you on yours?

PARTICIPATE

Chances are, while you've been reading this chapter you've already been thinking about someone you haven't forgiven. If you don't forgive, it will have an effect on your life. Take time to walk through the BluePrint. Consider the REST the Father has offered you. Think of all you've put on the table. Abide in prayer, consider how you can obey God's word, Listen for what the Spirit is saying regarding this potential forgiveness and how could you practice forgiveness? Make a plan to forgive, and nail it down.

BUILD

Turn to the Week #7 Scriptures in the back of the book and read each passage on the coinciding day.

Continue reading Page Eight of the BluePrint now, or come back in a week after going through all of Week #7's scriptures.

To build on the BluePrint, consider putting a reminder in your calendar or phone for every Thursday called "Today is a day to Forgive as I've Been Forgiven."

The BluePrint

The BluePrint

Chapter Ten: BluePrint Page Eight
WORK with God

The first real job I had was at The Fort Armstrong in downtown Rock Island, IL. The Fort is a retirement village where I washed dishes and served in the dining hall. When I say I was a server, I mean I picked up the previously requested meals in the kitchen and took them to the table with the same number as the order. It wasn't difficult. It was an ok job. I didn't love it, but I really liked driving to work.

There was a major S-curve in one of the roads on the way to work where 5th Avenue would curve hard to the right and then hard back to the left becoming 4th Avenue, dropping you into downtown Rock Island. I was 16, so obviously I would drive through the curve as fast as I could in my rusted out brown two-door 1984 Toyota Celica. It was awesome. The curve. Not the car.

Now I'm a pastor at a church right here in Rock Island, and what's crazy is that we're currently (as of the writing of this chapter) rehabbing the building on that very same S-curve to be our new church home. It's funny how an S-curve I would speed through as fast as I could will now be the corner I carefully slow down on and turn off of so I can pastor God's people to REST, LIVE, and WORK in a great House.

I think this is a good picture for what our work with God can be. Instead of being hurried, we can slow down and find our call and purpose hiding right on the corner of what we were speeding past. I wasn't just in a hurry, I wasn't paying attention. When I was 16 years old, I never even noticed there was a building there. I was just on my way to work to get a job done. How often are we missing what God has for us because we're moving too fast, looking right past it, just trying to get something done?

Open your Bible to John 13:3-15. There's this moment in John 13 when Jesus is washing his disciples' feet and specifically tells them that he's setting an example of how we should work. He says, "Do as I have done." But Peter almost missed it. Peter actually tells Jesus he doesn't want to let him wash his feet. It's like Peter says, "move on Jesus, go to the next guy. Not me. If anything, I should be washing your feet." But Jesus makes a pretty cut and dry statement about why it's necessary. This is the way I hear Jesus saying it, "Peter, you're missing what is happening. I'm showing you how to work. To work is to serve, and to be served is to receive what you need. I'm giving you something I have, and if you don't receive this from me, how will you in turn give it away?"

Jesus says and shows that the way we work comes from what we receive. Work is meant to offer the rest and life that we've received to others that still don't have it.

So in the BluePrint, what is work? Work is offering rest and life to others. And work comes last, after rest and living at the table, after abiding in prayer and obeying God's word, after listening to the Spirit and practicing our faith, and after forgiving as we have been forgiven. The BluePrint of discipleship is designed this way so that we don't work from ourselves, but from everything that God has for us.

And this is so important, because the way we offer life and rest is actually the embodiment of God's message. The way you work with God is probably the single greatest example to those around you of what God is really about.

When I was in the 8th grade my best friend was named David and he wasn't a Christian. I remember a specific moment when we stood in the hallway outside my bedroom and I told him about Jesus. Through tears I pleaded with him. I remember wanting so badly for him to believe in Jesus, but he never did. About 10 years later we reconnected and I learned he had become a Christian. I worked up the nerve to ask him why he never chose to believe in Jesus when I would ask him. He said something along the lines of, "it seemed like it was more about you than Jesus."

How you work with God matters. If you work frantically, what will people believe about God? If you work from duty, or legalism, or drive, what will people believe about God? If you procrastinate, put off, or forget to do what God has called you to do, what will people believe about God?

How we work matters. But how do you

know what your work is?

I have a very simple exercise for you. A prayer, really. If work is offering rest and life to others, and if our work is offering what we have already received, then here is a prayer to explore how we should work with the Spirit of God.

Pray this prayer: God, what have you put in me or want to call out of me that will offer rest and life to others?

It's as simple as that. If you take the time to pray, to abide in prayer and ask God this question, he will be faithful in answering. I believe that resting in God, living at the table, abiding in prayer, obeying God's word, listening to the Spirit, practicing your faith, and forgiving as you have been forgiven, will all lead you to hear clearly from God the answer to this prayerful question: God, what have you put in me or want to call out of me that will offer rest and life to others?

PARTICIPATE

Prayer for Work

Oh God of meaningful work
We have labored so often for the wrong reasons. To get, To achieve, To advance
Our work has been marred by our sin
Clean it up. Make it right again
From a place of rest and life, show us how to work again for your glory, for your name, for your sake
Give us meaningful work that leads again to meaningful rest. Amen.

BUILD

Read Week #8 Scriptures on the coinciding day.

Continue to the last chapter of the BluePrint now, or come back next week.

Put a reminder in your calendar or phone for every Thursday called "Today is a day to WORK with God"

The BluePrint

The BluePrint

Chapter Eleven: the BluePrint's Final Page
Your Home Inspection

Jason Rivera will inspect your home, if you live in California. He's a great friend of mine, and because he's the best, you can be sure you'll know everything you need to know about the condition of your home when he's done. But Jason probably won't fly out to inspect your spiritual home, even if you tell him I sent you. Or maybe he would. Look him up.

Jason was my intern for a year at New Life Church in Colorado Springs while he was in the School of Worship and I was the Director of the Small Groups department. I loved the time we had together and we became great friends.

I'm mentioning Jason because I learned something important about myself because of him. I've inspected my spiritual life and found I am most like Jesus when I'm discipling someone. It was no different with Jason. We'd get coffee. We'd worship and write songs together. He'd sit in for important meetings and give me insight. We'd have dinner with each other's families. We'd talk about Jesus and what they thought God might have planned for us.

Years later Jason still loves Jesus with his whole heart, he leads his family well, he's in the worship band at his local church, and he can inspect your home at a reasonable rate. And *I'm* the better for it.

It's true. I'm most like Jesus when I'm intentionally discipling someone. I know this about myself, so I'm always looking for someone that wants to be discipled. But how do you learn about you? How do you know the condition of your house?

To assist you, I've created a basic Home Health Inspection you can take at the end of this chapter. You'll simply rate each area of the BluePrint in your life and you'll see more clearly what is deficient, what is doing well, and what is strong. Then you can go back to the corresponding chapters for insight on how to strengthen the areas of your BluePrint that need to grow.

But there's one other inspection I want to bring your attention to. It's the Toxicity Level Inspection. Every one of us runs the risk of getting stuck in REST, LIVE, or WORK, by giving one of these areas of relationship with God the kind of attention that can become detrimental to the others.

I believe there are specific toxic markers you can see when you're stuck in one area at the expense of the others. In REST, it's Atrophy. In LIVE, it's Entitlement. In WORK, it's Resentment.

As great as rest is, it will become toxic if we stay there and only there. Why? Because when all we do is rest, we atrophy. This is true of our physical bodies, and I believe it's true about our spiritual lives as well.

Have you ever walked into a house that's been sitting empty for years? Even if it was sealed off from the elements and the raccoons or squirrels haven't taken up residence in the attic, it still feels like something is wrong. It's eerie. Even though it looks fine, it feels dilapidated.

Somehow, a house, made of wood and brick, drywall and steel, has atrophied. You can feel it.

House flippers often pass on houses like this because after a few years you just don't know what might be wrong behind the walls or under the floorboards. Water pipes have been empty. Ventilation fans haven't been running. Toilets have gone unflushed. And this atrophy will happen to you too if you only rest.

On the other hand, a house lived in, with its dings and dents, feels more alive than a house untouched. You have to move forward and live. But what if we only live?

Have you ever been given everything you ever wanted? You'd think it would create a sense of thankfulness. Rather, it creates a sense of entitlement. It reminds me of a college party house where the party never stops. No one ever cleans or cares for the house because they think someone else will do it. They're there to receive, to have fun. And so this too becomes an unhealthy house.

When you go into a bookstore, this is what the religion bookshelf is filled with. Books on how to live. Self-help. Live in this aisle and you'll develop a toxic sense of entitlement. Live a Christian life that doesn't value rest or thinks that you're never required to do any work, and toxic entitlement will become your home. You have to move from live into work. But what if we only work?

I touched on this at the beginning of the book in the chapter on rest. If we never rest, if we don't live, and all we do is work, we will become resentful. Work is necessary to healthy discipleship, but if all we do is work, at some point it will get glazed in resentment.

Have you ever visited a house that was spotless? You were asked to remove your shoes when you came in. You weren't asked to use a coaster for your drink in the living room because before you had the chance, you were told not to leave the kitchen with any food or drinks. You brought your kids and they were asked to sit still the whole time, never offered any toys. So you thought you'd send them outside to the yard to play, only to be told to stay off the grass. The homeowner resented the very idea that you would even consider the risk of leaving a water ring on their table, or let your kids leave a toy on the carpet.

This is resentment: you assume no one

appreciates the work you've done, so you feel no sense of joy when they benefit from it. And when they do benefit, you treat them passive-aggressively as though they have no idea how hard you *really* worked, and that they wouldn't help clean up even if asked.

Sound familiar? It might be what you're feeling right now. Doesn't feel good does it? That's because it's toxic. But there's good news. There's a way out of toxicity. God will help you, and I believe the BluePrint is one tool he might want you to use to be revived and become healthy again.

My hope is that you have found great value in this book and that now you'll take both inspections on the following pages so you can find out what areas of the BluePrint could use some attention. Find out how much atrophy, entitlement, or resentment you might have built up. Then make the most of the BluePrint and grow!

I'll tell you this final bit of insight about the BluePrint. It sounds odd, but the path to strengthening your framework in the BluePrint is always to work backward. If you lack forgiveness, work backward and practice your faith. If you lack practicing, go back to listening. If you lack listening, go back to obeying. And so on. Don't build more on top until what is underneath is solid.

Conversely, the way to find your way out of a toxicity trap is to cycle forward. If you're stuck in rest/atrophy, cycle forward to live. Pray, read your Bible, and so on. If you're stuck in live/entitlement, cycle forward to work. Start to give back when all you've done is receive. If you're stuck in work/resentment, cycle back to the beginning and rest. Lay work aside, rest for a time, and then walk back through the pages of the BluePrint, so when you work again, it will be built on something solid.

I believe the greatest value of a BluePrint is in following every page without ignoring the others. You wouldn't try to build the second story of your house without digging the foundation first. Nor would you dig the foundation and only live there. If you want to grow, if you want to avoid toxicity, I encourage you to explore every page. I hope you see your faith being built.

I'll leave you with the prayer I pray every Sunday before we explore the word of God:

Father God, thank you for your word. I pray that today, whatever you have for us to learn, whatever you want us to remember, let it stick. Let it become a part of the framework of our faith. That our faith would become stronger. That we would become more like your son, Jesus. Amen.

Home Health Inspection
(a high total is healthier)

REST – I take time to rest, because of God
        1 2 3 4 5 6 7 8 9 10

LIVE – I trust God and others with my life
        1 2 3 4 5 6 7 8 9 10

Abide – I regularly spend time in prayer
        1 2 3 4 5 6 7 8 9 10

Obey – I regularly read the Bible
        1 2 3 4 5 6 7 8 9 10

Listen – I take time to hear the Spirit speak
        1 2 3 4 5 6 7 8 9 10

Practice – I act on what I believe about God
        1 2 3 4 5 6 7 8 9 10

Forgive – I forgive and don't hold grudges
        1 2 3 4 5 6 7 8 9 10

WORK – I serve and care for others freely
        1 2 3 4 5 6 7 8 9 10

Toxicity Level Inspection
(a low total is healthier)

Atrophy – I feel tired, like my spiritual growth has stalled. I say things like "I don't understand my Bible" or "I don't know how to pray" but never ask for help, and I give up easily.

    1 2 3 4 5 6 7 8 9 10

    Rarely --------------- Often

Entitled – I feel like I've not been given enough, and I'm bothered when I'm asked to give or serve. I say things like "I'm just not being fed" or "why doesn't the pastor approach me?"

    1 2 3 4 5 6 7 8 9 10

    Rarely --------------- Often

Resentful – I'm regularly frustrated and feel unappreciated for my work. I say things like "I didn't sign up for this," or "If I don't do it, who will?"

    1 2 3 4 5 6 7 8 9 10

    Rarely --------------- Often

The BluePrint

The BluePrint

BluePrint Daily Bible Verse Plan

WEEK #1	DAY	VERSE
REST	Saturday	Matthew 11:28
LIVE at the Table	Sunday	Luke 22:19-20
Abide in Prayer	Monday	Matthew 6:6
Obey God's Word	Tuesday	Matthew 4:4
Listen to the Spirit	Wednesday	John 16:13
Practice Your Faith	Thursday	Matthew 5:14-16
Forgive as Forgiven	Friday	Matthew 5:44
WORK	Any Day	Genesis 1:1-10

WEEK #2	DAY	VERSE
REST	Saturday	John 14:27
LIVE at the Table	Sunday	1 Thessalonians 5:11
Abide in Prayer	Monday	Colossians 4:2
Obey God's Word	Tuesday	Psalms 119:10-11
Listen to the Spirit	Wednesday	John 14:16-17, 26
Practice Your Faith	Thursday	Romans 12:6-8
Forgive as Forgiven	Friday	Matthew 18:21-22
WORK	Any Day	Psalm 127:1

BluePrint Daily Bible Verse Plan

WEEK #3	DAY	VERSE
REST	Saturday	Isaiah 30:15
LIVE at the Table	Sunday	Ecclesiastes 4:9-12
Abide in Prayer	Monday	Hebrews 4:16
Obey God's Word	Tuesday	2 Timothy 3:16-17
Listen to the Spirit	Wednesday	Acts 1:8
Practice Your Faith	Thursday	Matthew 7:7-8
Forgive as Forgiven	Friday	Romans 12:18-20
WORK	Any Day	Acts 20:35

WEEK #4	DAY	VERSE
REST	Saturday	Proverbs 19:23
LIVE at the Table	Sunday	Hebrews 10:24-25
Abide in Prayer	Monday	Philippians 4:6-7
Obey God's Word	Tuesday	Romans 15:4
Listen to the Spirit	Wednesday	Romans 8:14, 26-27
Practice Your Faith	Thursday	Proverbs 18:16
Forgive as Forgiven	Friday	Ephesians 4:26, 32
WORK	Any Day	Galatians 6:9

BluePrint Daily Bible Verse Plan

WEEK #5	DAY	VERSE
REST	Saturday	Psalm 62:1-2
LIVE at the Table	Sunday	Colossians 3:16
Abide in Prayer	Monday	1 Thessalonians 5:16-18
Obey God's Word	Tuesday	Hebrews 4:12
Listen to the Spirit	Wednesday	Mark 13:11
Practice Your Faith	Thursday	Ephesians 4:11-12
Forgive as Forgiven	Friday	Colossians 3:13
WORK	Any Day	Ephesians 2:10

WEEK #6	DAY	VERSE
REST	Saturday	Philippians 4: 6-7
LIVE at the Table	Sunday	2 Corinthians 13:11
Abide in Prayer	Monday	Psalm 18:6
Obey God's Word	Tuesday	Psalms 1:1-2
Listen to the Spirit	Wednesday	Acts 10:15-20
Practice Your Faith	Thursday	Colossians 3:23-24
Forgive as Forgiven	Friday	1 Peter 3:9
WORK	Any Day	Philippians 2:14-1

BluePrint Daily Bible Verse Plan

WEEK #7	DAY	VERSE
REST	Saturday	1 Peter 5:7
LIVE at the Table	Sunday	Acts 2:42-47
Abide in Prayer	Monday	Psalm 145:18
Obey God's Word	Tuesday	2 Timothy 2:15
Listen to the Spirit	Wednesday	Galatians 4:6-7
Practice Your Faith	Thursday	1 Peter 4:10-11
Forgive as Forgiven	Friday	1 John 1:9
WORK	Any Day	Colossians 3:17

WEEK #8	DAY	VERSE
REST	Saturday	Exodus 33:14
LIVE at the Table	Sunday	Proverbs 27:17
Abide in Prayer	Monday	1 John 5:14
Obey God's Word	Tuesday	James 1:22
Listen to the Spirit	Wednesday	1 Corinthians 2:14
Practice Your Faith	Thursday	2 Corinthians 8:8-9
Forgive as Forgiven	Friday	1 Thessalonians 5:15
WORK	Any Day	James 2:17

The BluePrint

PRAYER OF BECOMING*

Oh patient and always-loving God, thank you for making space for us to become more like you

You don't stand over us barking orders and demanding daily improvement

You live within us, daily speaking grace and guidance

We are becoming more like you because this is what you do, you make the old, new

You make the dead, alive

You make the broken, whole

You make us like your son Jesus

You make us like you

Amen.

*The prayers of Belonging, REST, LIVE, WORK, and Becoming, were first published in The House – a Local Church's *Local Book* given to each new guest at The House. Also found on Amazon.